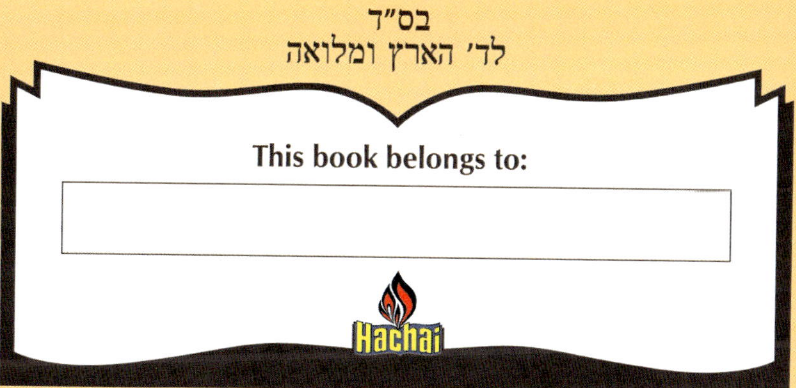

Please read it to me!

The Key under the Pillow

A Story about Honoring Parents

by Leah Perl Shollar
illustrated by Harvey Klineman

Adapted from Talmud Bavli
Kiddushin 31/A, including Rashi and Tosfos

For my parents who provided a living example of Kibbud Av V'eim, and for my in-laws who raised a mentch. With gratitude to Avinu Sh'bashamaim. L.P.S.

In honor of my parents. H.K.

The Key Under the Pillow

First Edition - Sivan 5764 / June 2004

Editor - Devorah Leah Rosenfeld
Layout - Eli Designs

Paperback Edition 5779 / 2019
ISBN: 978-1-945560-24-8

Hardcover Edition 5764 / 2004
ISBN: 978-1-929628-16-2
LCCN: 2003117063

HACHAI PUBLISHING
Brooklyn, New York
Tel: 718-633-0100 Fax: 718-633-0103
www.hachai.com - info@hachai.com

GLOSSARY

EIFOD - Vest; one of the eight garments worn by the Kohen Gadol while performing the service in the Holy Temple

HASHEM - G-d

KIBBUD AV V'EIM - (The commandment) to honor one's father and mother

KOHEN GADOL - High Priest

SHOHAM - Onyx

YERUSHALAYIM - Jerusalem

Dama slid down from the saddle and brushed the gritty sand from his clothing. His father, Nesina, swung open the front door. "Come in son, come in and refresh yourself."

Dama hugged his father and said, "My journey across the desert was worth the trouble. I've brought back the finest black onyx stones!"

Inside, Dama washed his face and hands while Nesina laid food on a tray.

"Father, please sit. I will serve you." Dama poured water and set a plate of salty cheese, glistening olives, and fresh bread in front of his father.

Only then did Dama sit down. He gulped mug after mug of cool, sweet water. "I feel much better now," he sighed.

Dama held up a small leather pouch. "Here, Father. Would you like to see?"

Nesina untied the pouch and poured the shiny black stones into his hand. The onyx gleamed smooth and glossy.

"Beautiful, Dama! You will fetch an exceptional price for these."

He poured the onyx back into the pouch and said, "I have been up since dawn waiting for your arrival. It is time for me to rest."

Dama helped his father up. He put his arm around Nesina's shoulders and walked with him to the quiet bedroom.

While Nesina settled down to rest, Dama opened the heavy wooden chest where he kept his gems.

He tucked the onyx in next to velvety blue sapphires, speckled jaspers, and wine-colored garnets. Dama locked the chest and pushed it back in place at the foot of the bed.

"Father, will you hide the key for me?"

Nesina slid it under his pillow.

"Your key is safe with me.

Don't worry."

Dama turned and hurried to his worktable, where a pile of uncut topaz awaited him. Using a small hammer and chisel, he chipped away bits of brown rock to uncover the smoky colored gems underneath.

But soon, sleep overtook him, and Dama's head nodded lower and lower against his shoulder.

A rap at the door woke him. He stretched and rubbed his eyes. Two men stood in the doorway, the bright sunlight behind them.

"May I help you?" asked Dama.

The elderly man with a long gray beard nodded.

"We seek Dama, the son of Nesina – the gem merchant."

"I am Dama." He bowed. "Please, come in."

Dama seated them on plump floor-cushions and brought a jug of cool water.

The elderly one leaned forward. "We are rabbis from Yerushalayim. We must replace the onyx-shoham stones in the Kohen Gadol's eifod-vest."

Dama nodded. "I happen to have some very choice pieces."

The elderly rabbi cradled two empty golden settings in the palms of his hands.

"Do you have any as large as these?"

Dama's face lit up. "I think I have the very jewels for you! They are of the best quality and just the right size."

"And the price?" asked the elderly rabbi.

Dama thought for a moment. "Six hundred thousand gold coins."

"Let us examine the stones," said the rabbi. "If they are as perfect as you say, we accept your price."

Dama's heart throbbed with excitement as he hurried to get the onyx.

Father will be amazed that I've sold the stones so quickly, and at such a good price! He stopped short, remembering that his father was asleep.

Then he waved away his worry. *Surely I can get the stones without waking him!*

Silently, Dama slipped the latch. Creak by creak, he pulled open the door.

Slowly, on tiptoe, he crept across the darkened room. It was quiet except for Nesina's soft breathing.

Dama's eyes went to the pillow. Maybe he could slide out the key!

Dama crept closer, but – what was this? His shoulders fell.

Nesina had stretched out so far that his feet lay upon the chest... the chest with the precious gems!

Dama watched Nesina's back rise and fall. *I've never made six hundred thousand gold coins in one day! Perhaps, just this once, I should wake my father? Should I?*

He stretched out his hand, then snatched it back. "No," he whispered. "I will not do it. Honoring Father is more important than making money for myself."

Dama tiptoed noiselessly from the room and hurried back to the rabbis.

"I'm sorry to have kept you waiting, but I cannot help you today. My father is asleep with his feet resting on the chest full of gems... and the key is under his pillow!"

The elderly rabbi raised his eyebrows and smiled. "For such a huge sum of money, I'm sure your father wouldn't mind if you woke him."

Dama shook his head.

The two rabbis whispered together. "Perhaps he just wants more money," said the young one. The elderly rabbi nodded and turned to Dama.

"What if we give you seven hundred thousand gold coins for the onyx?"

Dama sighed. "I'm sorry, I cannot accept."

The elderly rabbi spoke again, "Eight hundred thousand gold coins. It's our final offer."

Dama gasped. *That's a fortune! I could buy hundreds of gems with so much money. If I don't wake my father right away, they will surely go to another gem merchant.*

Dama took a deep breath. "All my life I have been careful never to call my father by his name, never to sit in his place – and never to wake him from his sleep."

For a full moment, there was silence. Finally, the elderly rabbi spoke. "Your honor for your father is worth more than gems. For such devotion you will certainly be rewarded! As for us, we must seek our stones elsewhere."

After the rabbis left, Dama sat down heavily at his work table. "I lost a lot of money today," he thought, "and who knows if I will ever be rewarded?" He shrugged. "But I do know I was right not to wake Father."

Dama sold many gemstones in the months that followed, but none for as much money as the rabbis had been willing to pay.

Month followed month, and a whole year passed. One morning, Dama strode to the barn, bucket in hand, to milk the cows.

Inside, his black cow lay in the straw. Nuzzled against her side was a tiny newborn heifer – entirely red!

“Father!” He poked his head around the door of the barn. “Please come quickly! Have you ever seen anything so strange?”

Nesina was amazed. “I’ve heard that red cows are very valuable. Maybe those rabbis you told me about would be interested in this.”

Dama sent a messenger to Yerushalayim, and waited eagerly for a reply. Before long, the rabbis returned – this time with a caravan of wagons.

Dama led the way to the grassy slope where his herd grazed. Nesina stood waiting with the red heifer.

Each of the rabbis examined the little cow from her head to her hooves, checking every hair. All red! They looked at each other. The older one smiled and tugged on his beard. The younger one nodded his head in wonder.

"A completely red heifer is very rare," he said. "In the history of the world, only ten will ever be born. And you have one!"

The elderly rabbi spoke. "Dama, this red heifer is surely your reward for honoring your father. She's worth more than the finest gem. Please tell us your price."

"Now that I know my red heifer is so important to you," Dama answered, "I could charge all the money in the world. But I don't want anything except the gold coins I lost by not waking my father."

"Do you mean the eight hundred thousand coins?" asked the elderly rabbi.

"No," said Dama. "I mean the six hundred thousand we first agreed upon. It was a fair price."

The rabbi clasped Dama's hand and led him to one of the wagons. He pulled back the cover to reveal a mountain of golden coins, glinting and glittering in the sun.

Dama scooped up a handful and let them run through his fingers. He shook his head. He blinked. Slowly a smile spread across his face. Dama twirled around, shouting and laughing, then danced over to Nesina and threw his arms around his father.

The younger rabbi turned to the older one. "Ask me how much we must do to honor our parents, and I will forever point to the deeds of a man named Dama, the son of Nesina."

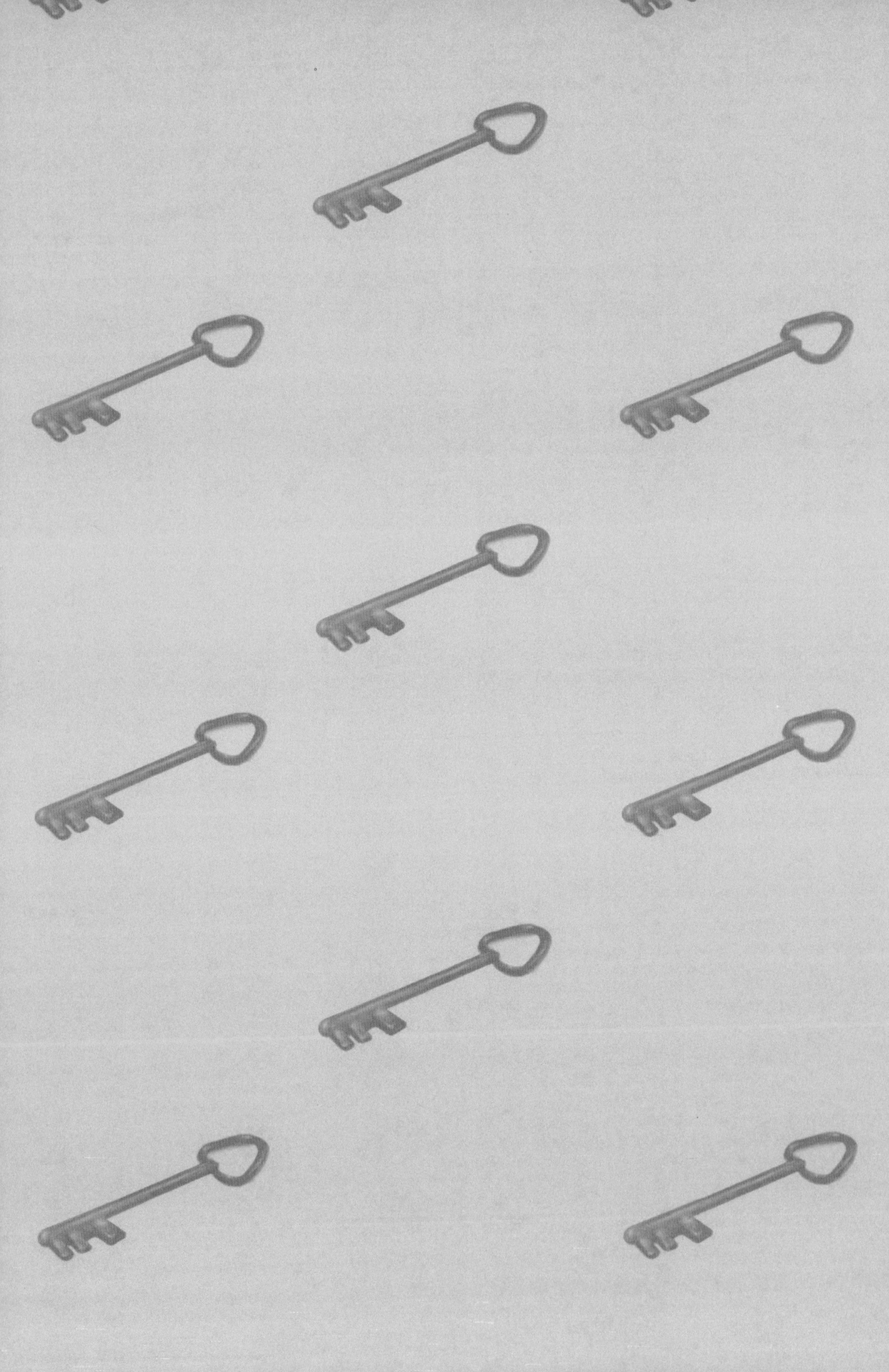

NOTE:

The very first 'Parah Adumah,' (red heifer) was used in the days of Moshe (Moses) to purify the nation following Miriam's death.[1] From that time, until the destruction of the Second Temple thousands of years later, only nine heifers met the stringent requirements.[2] A heifer could not qualify if it had even two black hairs, had ever borne a yoke on its neck, or carried anything on its back.[3]

Rabbi Moshe ben Maimon (Maimonides) tells us that the tenth and final red heifer will be prepared when the anointed king of the Jews, Moshiach, comes. 'May he speedily be revealed, Amen; so may be the will of Hashem.'[4]

---

[1] Bamidbar 20:1, Rashi [2] Parah 3:5 [3] Bamidbar 19:2, Rashi; Parah 2:5
[4] Hilchos Parah Adumah 3:4

Made in the USA
Middletown, DE
14 February 2022

61143397R00022